so you want to
write
Fiction

Tony Bradman

HODDER
Wayland

A division of Hodder Headline Limited

Other title in the series:

So You Want To Write Poetry

Text © Tony Bradman 2003
Editor: Gill Munton
Designer: Sarah Borny

Published in Great Britain in 2003 by Hodder Wayland,
an imprint of Hodder Children's Books

The website addresses (URLs) included in this book were valid at
the time of going to press. However, because of the nature of the Internet,
it is possible that some addresses may have changed, or sites may have
changed or closed down since publication. While the author and Publisher
regret any inconvenience this may cause readers, no responsibility for any
such changes can be accepted by either the author or the Publisher.

A Catalogue record for this book is available from the British Library.

ISBN: 07502 36477(hb)
07502 38593 (pb)

Printed in Hong Kong

Hodder Children's Books
A division of Hodder Headline Limited
338 Euston Road, London NW1 3BH

I'd like to thank all the writers who spared their valuable
time to answer my questions and talk to me about writing.
This book wouldn't have been the same without them!

Tony Bradman

Contents

Introduction

So you want to write fiction? Well, that's no surprise – in fact, writing stories is a completely natural thing for you to do.

People have always loved making up stories. It probably started with our remote ancestors sitting round the fire in their caves, telling each other stories to while away the long, dark evenings before television was invented. Some even painted picture stories on cave walls – the first comic strips! Once the story genie was out of the bottle, though, it grew and grew ...

Myths and legends, epic poems and fairytales all existed long before anyone wrote them down. But it was with the invention of printing that stories really took off. Today, millions of picture books, short story collections and novels – the stuff we collectively call fiction – are printed and read every year.

Surrounded by stories

Stories appear in other forms, too. These days you could almost say that we're surrounded by stories. There are comics, cartoons and graphic novels, films, radio plays and story tapes, television plays, serials and soaps. Many of us spend a huge amount of time reading, listening to or watching stories – and then discussing them at length with our friends and families.

Why do we all love stories?

They're great fun, of course, even – or especially – when they're scary. That's certainly what made me become a writer. I discovered books at my local library when I was young, and found I liked reading stories so much, I ended up wanting to write some myself!

But there's another reason why everybody likes stories   perhaps a rather more important one. I believe that good stories can help us to understand ourselves and other people better, and can even help us to deal with our problems.

Our bear was quite bowled over by the story. It was funny and sad, and utterly persuasive. He listened as though his life depended on it. He was desperate to know what the end would be, and hoping that the end would never come …

**From *The Bear That Nobody Wanted*
by Allan Ahlberg**

Don't worry if you think that's a big claim – I'll be coming back to it later on. For now I'll be concentrating on the nuts and bolts of writing stories, to help you with your own writing:

- **How to get good story ideas and develop them**

- **How to give your stories great beginnings, middles and endings**

- **How to create believable, interesting characters**

- **How to develop a plot**

- **How to establish a theme**

- **How to develop a style**

And the best place to start is with the basic ingredients of any story. There are two, and to find out what they are you'll have to turn to the next page … (That's what we writers call suspense – see page 25 for more details!)

The basic ingredients

Of course, we all know what goes into a story – or do we? What makes a piece of writing a story? It's made up, invented, of course. But apart from that, I believe that there are two basic ingredients, and that if what you're writing doesn't have both, it isn't a story:

- **A story must have a character (or characters). Stories are *about* somebody.**

- **A problem must be posed in a story. Stories are about things going wrong.**

All kinds of character

You've probably encountered a vast range of characters in the stories you've read – ordinary children, boy wizards, giants with enormous ears, sheep who want to be dogs, talking toads, fairies, monsters – even teachers! And I've written stories featuring all kinds of character – kids, grown-ups, Egyptian mummies, aliens, gerbils, a family of dinosaurs, a giant killer bogie …

I can even imagine writing a story about a stone. But if that stone was just a stone, and didn't have thoughts or feelings, the story wouldn't be very interesting, would it? And that's the point. Characters in stories are always people like you and me, even if they're disguised as animals or robots.

Problems to be solved

Characters aren't enough in themselves, though. They need problems to deal with, or there will be no story. Take a character like Harry Potter, for example. Would we be interested in reading books about Harry if he was an ordinary boy from a nice, ordinary family who went to a nice, ordinary school where nothing exciting happened? Er … I don't think so.

But Harry does have lots of problems to face, and there are more to tackle when his solutions go wrong, or when things happen as a result of his actions. And with each new problem, we're drawn further and further into the story.

Sometimes, a problem is disguised as a good thing. For example, a character may be given three wishes, or find hidden treasure. What matters is that the character's life is changed in a way that's going to cause trouble. Wishes go wrong; the bandits who own the treasure want it back – and soon our character is being forced to deal with one tricky situation after another.

THE STORY
The BFG
by Roald Dahl

THE PROBLEM
Sophie is kidnapped by a big-eared giant in the middle of the night, and taken to a strange land …

THE STORY
The Machine Gunners
by Robert Westall

THE PROBLEM
During the Second World War, some children take a machine gun from a crashed German plane, and put themselves in deadly danger …

7

Coming up with ideas

Where do you get your ideas? That's probably the question writers are asked most often. I asked Allan Ahlberg (author of *The Bear That Nobody Wanted*) where he got his ideas, and he said:

I'm a bit like a tap. I just seem to turn on my mind, and ideas for all sorts of things pour out – poems, picture books, stories, novels ...
Allan Ahlberg

So that's it, then, you might think. Writers are special, the kind of people who just have loads of ideas. Hang on a minute, though – let's look again at what Allan said. "I just seem to turn on my mind, and ..." I talked to Jeremy Strong, too, and he said: "Ideas can come from anywhere, especially if I'm in the right, receptive kind of mood."

Ideas are all around us

The truth is that ideas for stories are all around us. Most writers keep a notebook and a pen with them all the time so they can jot down ideas before they forget them.

Many writers will tell you that they get ideas from strange, unusual or just plain interesting things they see people doing, or something they suddenly remember, or read about, or stumble across while they're channel hopping. The difference is that writers look out for these things, and then start asking themselves questions.

For instance, a few years ago I was watching a favourite film of mine, the first (black-and-white) version of *Frankenstein*. I found myself thinking what an interesting character the monster was. Then I asked myself, what if the monster got a job and became someone ordinary, like … a teacher? And if he did become a teacher, what could go wrong for him? Maybe the children in his class would be frightened of him. But what if they weren't? What if the monster was sweet and gentle, and it was the children who were horrible, making fun of him because he was ugly?

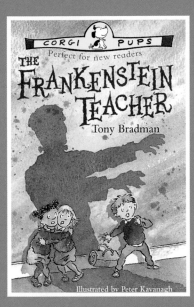

That chain of questions and answers eventually became one of my most successful books, *The Frankenstein Teacher*. Once I'd thought of the character, it was really just a question of coming up with interesting problems for him to face – and one thing led to another.

You can do it, too. Keep your eyes and ears (and your mind!) open, and when something strikes you as interesting or strange or funny, think about what it might mean to a character in a story. Then ask yourself some questions – and give your character a tough time!

Soon you'll find you've got the makings of a good story. But there's a long way to go …

> **TOP TIP:** One way of giving a character a problem to solve is to dump him or her in a completely new situation. A Frankenstein monster becomes a teacher, an adult is turned into a child, a wizard finds that he's lost his powers. Television writers call this a "Fish out of water" story.

"I like to have lots of ideas for stories – I jot them all down in my diary and think about them carefully. Generally, one idea takes over and I concentrate on it … I got the idea for Tracey Beaker when I saw several haunting adverts of children in care, smiling desperately at the camera under captions like "Do you want to look after me?" I just wondered what it would be like to be advertised like that.

Jacqueline Wilson

Developing your idea

OK, you've got an idea – a character with a problem (or several problems!) to deal with. So now it's time to start writing, right? Well … maybe, and maybe not. Some writers do just dive in and start scribbling like mad (or pounding on a keyboard). Others, however, get to this point … and stop.

That's what Philip Ridley (author of *Scribbleboy* and *Krindlekrax*) always does:

If I get a really good idea, I put it on a sort of mental back burner. I just let it bubble in a cooking pot at the back of my mind while I get on with other things. Then suddenly … the pot will boil over!

Philip Ridley

Adèle Geras (author of *Troy*) sometimes thinks about an idea for a couple of years, imagining the story that might grow from it, developing it and thinking about the characters and events it might involve:

> **That's the most enjoyable part of the whole process. It's rather like playing.**

Adèle Geras

That's exactly how I feel about the development stage, too. It's when you can let your imagination take flight – when you can dream up what kind of world your characters might live in, what their problems might be, what they might do to solve them, what happens next and how they might react …

I like to think of this as daydreaming with a purpose. The point is to discover where your story might take you, to find out which bits fit with other bits, to give you lots of material for when it comes to doing the actual writing.

You can start making some important decisions at this stage, too. Is your story going to be short or long? Funny or scary? Realistic or a fantasy? Is it for all ages, or for a specific age range? From whose point of view will the story be told? (That's a subject we'll come back to a little later – see page 19.)

Some writers like to plan their stories, sometimes in great detail, while others don't. I'm definitely a planner – during the "daydreaming with a purpose" stage, I start making notes (in big notebooks) about every aspect of the story, and gradually a rough plan (or outline) begins to emerge.

The plan is only there as a guide, though. It often changes once I get into the story, especially if the story is a long one with several characters and lots of things happening.

11

Beginnings

You've got your character, and you may have a plan for where you want your story to go. But how do you start it?

Well, you could introduce your main character, describing him or her and setting the scene so that the reader knows where the action is going to take place. Then there are the other characters to be described, things to be explained …

Hold on a minute – that's a lot of description and explanation, isn't it? You could write pages and pages before anything actually happens. But isn't that what we're looking for when we read stories – interesting things happening? And the sooner it all starts happening the better – right? It won't, though – not until you introduce the second basic ingredient – a problem.

One of my favourite books is *Charlotte's Web* by E.B. White. It's the story of a little girl called Fern, who lives on a farm, and this is how it begins:

SOME GREAT OPENING LINES

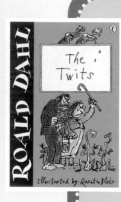

What a lot of hairy-faced men there are around nowadays!

**From *The Twits*
by Roald Dahl**

When Mary Lennox was sent to Misselthwaite Manor to live with her uncle, everybody said she was the most disagreeable-looking child ever seen.

**From *The Secret Garden*
by Mary Hodgson Burnett**

"Where's Papa going with that axe?" said Fern to her mother as they were setting the table for breakfast.

"Out to the hoghouse," replied Mrs. Arable …

In the next few lines we learn that a litter of piglets has just been born, and that one of them is small and weak. Fern's father has decided to "do away with it". Fern shrieks, and – before the bottom of the first page – she runs out of the house to stop her father killing the piglet.

Now that's what I call a good beginning. It introduces the main character, gives her a real problem to solve, and does the most important thing – it hooks the reader.

Another good thing about the beginning of *Charlotte's Web* is that it plunges the reader straight into the action. The characters are already talking, and things are happening. It's like getting on to a rollercoaster that's already moving. You gather information as you rattle along. You discover that Fern is the kind of person who thinks that it's wrong to kill a piglet just because it's small and weak, and that her father doesn't agree. So there's probably going to be plenty of conflict (see page 23) about the piglet, now, and later in the story.

Of course, not all stories start in that way. Some do begin with description and explanation. That's fine – as long as it hooks the reader, and as long as we get to some action as soon as possible!

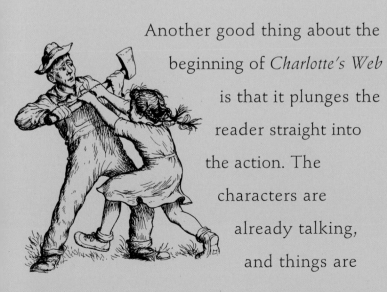

> **The first five words are the hardest part of a story to write ...**
> *Adèle Geras*

Middles

Right, you've started your story. You've introduced a main character and given him or her a problem to solve. So from here on it's easy, you may think. All you have to do now is make sure that a succession of things happen to the characters, and your story will be utterly brilliant …

Or will it? Not if it's just "things happening to the characters". The reader will soon get bored if the characters – particularly the main one – don't do anything to try and solve the problem. And if you really want to hold the reader's interest, the problem has to get worse before it gets better.

To illustrate what I mean, I'm going to use another story of mine, "Dilly and the Bike" (from *Dilly to the Rescue)*. I've written lots of stories about a young dinosaur called Dilly, but the central character in "Dilly and the Bike" is Dorla, Dilly's sister. Dorla's got a new bike, and her problem is that Dilly keeps pestering her for a ride on it. Dorla tries to sneak out for a ride without telling Dilly. He chases after her and they argue. Their father tells them off and sends them both to their rooms. When Dorla says she's sorry and asks if she can go out on her bike, her father says yes – but only if she takes Dilly with her.

Then Dilly reveals that he's discovered something about Dorla that she won't want their father to know, and he uses his knowledge to blackmail Dorla into letting him have a ride on her bike. Soon, Dorla is almost Dilly's slave …

The point is that Dorla keeps trying to do something about her problem – to escape Dilly's pestering, and enjoy riding her bike alone. But at every step of the way things get worse and worse for her.

The story would be boring if it were simply a series of arguments about the bike between Dorla and Dilly, but I made sure that there was a lot more to it than that. Things change, and develop, and become interestingly complicated. And that's what keeps the reader hooked, wanting to know how it all turns out.

The middle is almost certainly going to be the longest part of your story. If the story is a long one, you'll need to devise plenty of things your main character can do to try to solve the problem, and ways in which he or she just makes things worse! Plenty of surprises will help, too. In the story, Dorla doesn't expect Dilly to follow her when she sneaks out – and she doesn't expect to be blackmailed! Each time something surprising happens and the characters react, it takes your story to another level.

Endings

So, your story is rattling along and things are getting worse and worse for your main character – but how do you end it? You could just stop writing, but that probably wouldn't give you a good ending, and that's what we all want from a story. Another way of putting it is that we want a satisfying resolution.

There's really only one way to achieve that. Remember what I said about the basic ingredients of a story? That there are two, a character and a problem?

Well, you get a satisfying resolution when the character's problem is solved.

That's easy enough, you may think. In my story *The Frankenstein Teacher*, for example, the problem is that Mr. Frankenstein is desperate to be a good teacher and to be liked by the kids – but they just keep making fun of his ugliness.

I could have solved his problem by simply making the head teacher tell the kids to be nicer to him. This would have been one way of ending the story – but not a very good one. A better idea would be for the children in Mr. Frankenstein's class to learn that there's a lot more to him than his ugly exterior – and that someone's appearance is unimportant, anyway.

The climax of the story comes when Hannibal the class hamster is run over by a car, and Mr. Frankenstein plays the key role in getting him brought back to life. At that moment, the children see what a nice monster he is, and soon realise that he's actually the best teacher in the world.

In many good stories there's a major crisis before the ending. Things get worse and worse until it seems they're about as bad as they can be. This is the point at which Harry Potter has to face his greatest fear

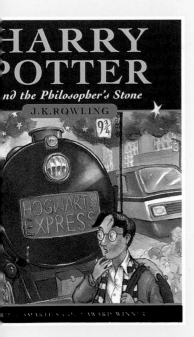

in the shape of Lord Voldemort, or Babe has to prove that he really can be a sheep-pig. It's the point at which

characters think they're going to be defeated or killed, or fail to fulfil their quest or to achieve their heart's desire. Through their difficulties, the characters have probably learned something about themselves and others, and have become stronger.

Of course, not all stories have happy endings. Sometimes the right ending is a sad one – the problem is solved, but at a cost. The key test of an ending is that the reader should feel that the story is over, leaving no loose ends – although a good story may leave you thinking about its characters for a while.

Giving life to your characters

Helen Dunmore

Most writers agree that characters are the main aspect of any story. After all, it will be very hard to keep your readers gripped if they're not interested in the characters you've created. Helen Dunmore, who's written many books for both children and adults, told me that she thinks "a writer needs to take time to know the characters – the villains as well as the heroes – as if they were close friends or family ..."

Forming a mental picture

Most of this should be done in the early stages of writing, when you're still developing your idea. A good way to do it is to ask yourself questions: How do the characters live? How do they speak? How do they laugh? What kind of food do they like? Are they tidy or untidy? Do they have any enemies?

In this way, you will gradually create a mental picture of your characters. Melvin Burgess (author of *The Baby and Fly Pie* and *Bloodtide*) calls it "understanding how your characters work", and Adèle Geras says that "once you hear them talking in your head, they come alive much more easily".

I haven't said that you need to come up with a complete, perfect description of what your characters *look* like. It's helpful to have some sort of description, but the truth is that in most stories the details of a character's appearance don't matter a great deal. We're interested in Harry Potter's courage and resourcefulness – not the colour of his hair or eyes!

Coming to life through action

Most writers say that characters only start to become themselves as they write the story. Characters come to life through their actions and words, the things they do to solve the problems they face.

Your characters should be consistent (without being boring); like real people, they should act in ways which are believable for their personalities.

"I don't know how I create characters. I suppose it's just like inventing imaginary friends when you're little. Characters do sometimes veer off in different directions and behave surprisingly – but that's half the fun of writing fiction."

Jacqueline Wilson

You can tell your story from different points of view:

FIRST PERSON
e.g. "I remember my first day at the school ..."

Advantage: The reader is right inside the character's head.

Disadvantage: You can include only the events which that character has experienced.

THIRD PERSON
e.g. "She ran into the forest ..."
Advantage: The reader is right inside the character's head.

Disadvantages: You can include only the events which that character has experienced. The text may feel a little distant.

UNIVERSAL THIRD PERSON
This is a general way of telling a story, revealing what all the characters think or feel.

Advantage: The reader can get inside the heads of all the characters.

Disadvantages: The story may jump around too much. The reader may not identify strongly with any of the characters.

Plot – the secret plan of your story

I mentioned plot earlier when I was talking about planning a story, and the two things are related. Many people think that "plot" is simply a fancy word for "plan", and that the two are identical. In fact, writers use the word "plot" because it has a very clear, specific meaning. People plot to commit a crime – think of Guy Fawkes and the Gunpowder Plot! That kind of plot is a plan, of course, but the key point is that it's a *secret* plan.

Drawing charts

Some writers work out their plots in detail, perhaps drawing charts to show what is going to happen in the story and what the reader should know at various stages. I've done that myself for certain stories. I've even gone back to the beginning of a story to put in some clues after I've written the ending!

Other writers like to concentrate on their characters and let the plot take care of itself.

Either way, the important thing is that the story should feel complete, with all the elements connected in some way.

> Character is much more important than plot. I don't work out plots in detail, and I wouldn't change a character to fit the plot.
>
> *Jacqueline Wilson*

The famous Greek philosopher Aristotle wrote a book about story writing in the fourth century BC. He thought that plot was very important, and that a good story should have a plot which starts with an action, goes through a series of connected events, and ends appropriately. The most important thing, he said, was the pattern of the events in the story.

Hiding clues

Surprises can make a story more interesting and exciting. But if those surprises are just new characters who suddenly appear, or things that happen without any explanation or preparation, your readers won't think much of the story. It will seem like a series of unconnected episodes.

Some of the best surprises involve a minor character doing something interesting that changes the course of the story. Alternatively, a fact that didn't seem important when you first read about it suddenly becomes an essential part of what happens.

In J.R.R. Tolkien's *The Lord of the Rings*, for instance, a character called Gollum is briefly mentioned in an early chapter. He seems like a fairly minor character in what is a massive story (over 1,000 pages!) In fact, Gollum plays a vital role in the story's resolution. When you read the ending, you're surprised by what Gollum does, but then you realise how right it is that he should do it. Writers create that kind of surprise by hiding clues in their stories.

Theme - what's your story about?

Good stories can help us to understand ourselves and others, and can even help us to deal with our problems. By now, you've probably begun to understand why. If stories are about characters overcoming problems, seeing how they do it might be helpful to readers with similar difficulties.

That underlying sympathy with a character may explain much of the appeal of stories with realistic settings – in book form and on television soaps.

We enjoy observing people like us trying to get through their lives, dealing with the problems that crop up.

This can also apply to stories which do not have realistic settings. For example, although few of us will ever have to deal with being

A scene from the BBC's soap opera, EastEnders. Robbie is consoling Sonia after she has given up her baby for adoption.

transformed into a mouse or having to fight an evil wizard, there may be times in our lives when we need to be courageous or resourceful – just like the characters in adventure or fantasy stories.

A good story has something interesting or original to say about how the characters deal with their lives – or, to put it a different way, a good story has a theme.

Finding a theme

Some writers explore a theme as a way of finding an idea for a story. For instance, when my children were young, they seemed to argue with each other a lot. I decided to write some stories about Dilly the dinosaur, his sister Dorla and their parents, and the conflicts in their family.

Those stories have proved to be popular (although I say so myself!) because they have strong characters and they're funny – but also because they tackle a theme that most of us are interested in: how should we get along with our families? The stories are dramatised conflicts that I hope will be entertaining – but I also want them to make readers think, and to ask questions.

The idea of conflict lies at the heart of many stories and gives them their themes. It may be the inner conflict of someone with an impossible choice to make, a conflict between people who want different things, or the eternal conflict between good and evil …

Many writers discover the theme of a story only after it's been written, but tackling a strong theme – bullying, or loyalty, or the desire for revenge – can make for a very strong story, especially if you create believable, interesting characters and a gripping plot.

Writing style and special effects

Many people think that there should be something special about the words in which a story is written – the language. They think it should be fancy, or clever, or full of long words and complicated sentences. You could write like that, and sometimes you may really need a long word or a complicated sentence. But fancy language can ruin a story. Jim Henson, who created the Muppets, had a sign in his studio that sums up the best approach: "Simple is good".

An appropriate style

The most important thing is telling the story, and the best way of doing that is to think through what you want to write, and then to write it in as simple and direct a way as you can. It's best to limit each sentence to one thought, one thing happening, or one line of speech; don't try to cram too much in.

It's like making a mosaic – you add to it gradually, one simple piece at a time, and eventually it becomes something quite complex. Now you can see why it might help to have some idea of the whole shape of your story – however rough – before you start. It can affect the placing of each individual piece.

I find that it's useful to read aloud what I have written. In that way, I get a feel for the flow of the story, and can see whether it's making sense. It's especially important to read aloud any dialogue to see if it sounds like real people talking – although I'll be looking at dialogue later (see page 29).

Using special effects

There is one special effect that lies at the heart of all good storytelling – suspense. Keeping your readers in suspense means giving them just enough information to make them want to know what's going to happen next – and making them wait to find out the rest.

For instance, in a horror story you could write, "A monster came down the corridor and burst into the classroom." But it would be more effective to write, "They could hear something thudding down the corridor towards the classroom. It was getting closer, and closer, and closer. The door handle slowly turned …"

Stretching out a part of your story like that can really increase the reader's tension. The monster will be much more scary when it finally appears, because you've allowed the reader's imagination to do most of the work. It's just like waiting for Christmas – most of the fun is in the anticipation!

> **TOP TIP:**
> If you're writing comedy, you still need good characters and an interesting plot. You also have to make sure that the story is funny! Comedy is harder to write than serious prose. If it isn't funny, it doesn't work.

> **TOP TIP:**
> Use short sentences with plenty of verbs for action sequences. Vary the pace – slow things down and speed them up again. That makes for a much more interesting and exciting read!

Revising - polishing until it shines!

Some people think that a good writer can produce great stories without making any mistakes or getting stuck, and that his or her stories are fully formed and perfect in the first draft. The truth is that very few of even the best writers can do that. Most writers learn through experience that a first draft can almost always be improved.

The habit of revising

I believe that the secret of learning how to be a good writer is understanding that revising your work shouldn't be a chore – it should be an essential part of the process of creating your story. After a while, you'll probably find that revising becomes a habit.

Revising is certainly built into the way I write. I think very hard about each sentence, each paragraph, each section of a story, and constantly rewrite. I have one principle in mind at all times: Does this line/sentence/paragraph/chapter work? That's the only test that matters. Does this sentence express what I want to say? Is this line of dialogue what this particular character would say at this stage in the story? Is there too much description? Should there be more action? Should I put in a clue here?

Every day when I start work, I go back over what I've written with these questions in mind. Then I write some new material, revising as I go along.

Drafting

Not all writers work like this. Some write a first draft without stopping. Then they revise the whole thing, producing a second draft. They may make further drafts. They may even move large chunks of the story around. Another word for "revising" is "editing" – a technical term for any work you do on a piece of writing to make it better.

Whichever way you work, you will end up with a fair copy – a final draft with which you are happy. I work on a computer (after the initial planning stage), and there's nothing I like more in my working life than to hear the sound of the printer churning out the pages of a story I've finished – especially when I know I've worked as hard as I could to make it good. I like to think that I've polished it until it shines!

I write by hand at least two drafts of a story, and then type it and revise the typescript two or three times. "If in doubt, cut it out" is my motto. I tend to love words too much, but I've discovered now that I can say what I want with fewer words. I'll become a poet in the end.

Michael Morpurgo

Revising, editing and polishing are vital. I write a first draft, immediately revise it, then print this off as a working draft. I will then rewrite completely at least once, often two, three or more times. But there are still small things which need changing. In fact, revising and polishing can be so enjoyable that I don't want to stop …

Helen Dunmore

Writing stories for other media

So far I've been writing about the stories you read in books – the kind generally known as prose fiction. There are several other media in which stories can appear, and each has special features.

Comics and graphic novels

The comic strip format is a visual medium. It tells stories through pictures, often relying on changes from frame to frame to show time passing or things happening. You can tell a story in a comic strip without any words of explanation at all, although most comic strip stories use speech bubbles and lines of narrative to help to move the story along (see example from *The Thing That Came From Jason's Nose*-right). And somebody will have decided who the characters are, and what should happen in the pictures and in which order. You do that by writing a script.

Everything I've said about stories also applies to comic strips. You still need a beginning, a middle and an end, and

you should bring your characters to life through their actions in an interesting series of events. Great pictures may enhance a story, but fantastic visuals for their own sake – just like fancy language in prose fiction – may distract attention from the story and lessen its impact.

Drama

Most other stories take the form of drama – stories designed to be acted out in words and action. There are plays, which you can see at a theatre or listen to on the radio; television drama (one-off plays, serials and soaps); and films (animations such as *Toy Story* or live action stories like *Harry Potter and the Philosopher's Stone*).

What I've said about stories applies to drama, too, but the important thing to remember is that in drama it's often much harder to get inside a character's mind.

Dialogue is therefore very important in drama. Not only does it have to keep the story moving, it also has to be right for the character who's saying it, and it must sound realistic (but not too realistic; in real life most people "um and ah", or repeat themselves).

SCENE 1   NIGHT

A TERRIFIC STORM IS RAGING. A FLASH OF LIGHTNING REVEALS A SPOOKY CASTLE ON A HILL, AND HITS A METAL ROD ON ITS ROOF. THE CAMERA MOVES TOWARDS A WINDOW, AND THEN GOES INSIDE. WE ENTER A LABORATORY FULL OF MACHINES. SPARKS ARE FLYING ...

THE DOCTOR IS STANDING BESIDE A RAISED BED – THE KIND THEY HAVE IN MORTUARIES – WHICH IS ATTACHED BY WIRES TO THE MACHINES. A SHEET COVERS SOMETHING SHAPED LIKE A MAN –BUT HUGE, AND STRANGE.

THE DOCTOR:
At last ... the moment I've been waiting for!

AS WE WATCH, THE SHAPE TWITCHES ...

THE DOCTOR:
Yes! My creation lives ...

THE SHAPE SITS UP AND THE SHEET FALLS AWAY. A HIDEOUS MONSTER IS REVEALED. IT GETS OFF THE BED AND STANDS. IT ADVANCES SLOWLY ON THE DOCTOR, MOANING AND GROANING.

THE DOCTOR:
Speak, my creature! What do you have to say?

THE MONSTER:
I ... want ... to ... be ... a teacher!

I believe having an ear for speech is like having an ear for music; some people are tone-deaf, others can carry a tune, and a few gifted writers have perfect pitch. And as with music, you can improve on what you've got – and in exactly the same way, too: by listening.

Greg Evans
scriptwriter for *The Bill* and *Casualty*

TV comes with pictures – you don't have to describe the way people talk, look, act. You don't have to describe the setting for your story.

Roy Apps
author and scriptwriter for *Byker Grove*

Where do you go from here?

So now you've got some idea of what makes a good story. The question is: Where do you go from here? Most writers would give you two simple answers:

- You can learn a lot about writing stories by reading (and watching) as many stories as possible.

- You can learn even more by writing your own stories, thinking carefully about what you're doing.

Reading and watching

Every professional writer I've ever met has been a great reader. Just as I did, they discovered in their childhood how wonderful stories are, and found that reading became a habit they couldn't imagine giving up. The more stories you read, the more you'll learn about the way in which stories work.

It's great to read for pleasure alone, and it's important to continue to enjoy stories. But if you really like a story, or find part of a story particularly exciting or gripping, it's worth going

"I learned my craft as a writer by reading and writing."
Melvin Burgess

back over it and trying to discover why it's so good.

And there's one very simple lesson I've learned from twenty years of being a writer: If you stick at it, one day you'll write a story that you know is good. There's no greater reward than that. So good luck – and keep on writing!

Glossary

character a person or animal represented in a story

dialogue the words spoken by characters in a story

draft a rough version of a story

first person a way of writing in which the main character refers to himself or herself (as "I")

graphic novel a long story which is presented in comic-strip format

narrative the telling of events in a story

pace the speed with which events are told in a narrative; the level of excitement in a narrative

plot a plan for a story

point of view the standpoint from which events can be seen; a story may be told from various points of view

prose a passage of written or spoken language which takes a non-poetical form

style the way in which an idea is expressed

theme the subject matter of a story; the idea behind a story

third person a way of writing in which the narrator refers to the characters as "he" or "she"

Index

Resources

Your writer's library

This should include a good dictionary and a thesaurus. A practical book on grammar and an encyclopedia would be useful, too.

Read the companion book to this, *So You Want To Write Poetry* by Brian Moses (Hodder Wayland).

Another excellent book is *The Book About Books* by Chris Powling (A & C Black). This tells you everything you've ever wanted to know about books, and has an excellent chapter on stories.

You could also try looking at *Writing for Children* by Allan Frewin Jones and Lesley Pollinger (Hodder & Stoughton). It's meant for grown-ups, but it's easy to read and has lots of great advice in it!

Favourite Writers by Kate Jones (Hodder Wayland) features interviews with a number of children's writers including David Almond, Quentin Blake, Malorie Blackman, Anne Fine, Roald Dahl, Michael Morpurgo, Terry Pratchett, Philip Pullman, JK Rowling, Jacqueline Wilson and Robert Swindells.

Make a collection of storybooks in a variety of styles. Try to read stories by all the writers mentioned in this book – and any others that take your fancy! You'll also find folk tales, myths and legends useful when you are learning about ways of storytelling – so look out for collections in your local library and at school.

Useful addresses

Magazines

Young Writer
Glebe House
Weobley
Herefordshire HR4 8SD

Tel: 01544 318901
Website: **www.mystworld.com/youngwriter**

This is a specialist magazine for young writers aged 6-16, featuring interviews with top children's writers and giving children opportunities to see their own prose and poetry in print. Three issues are published each year.

Wordsmith and **Scribbler**
c/o Young Writers
Remus House
Coltsfoot Drive
Woodston
Peterborough PE2 9JX

Tel: 01733 890066
e-mail: **youngwriters@forwardpress.co.uk**

Both magazines feature advice for young writers, interviews and opportunities for work to be published. *Wordsmith* is for children aged 12 and above, and *Scribbler* is for a younger readership. Both are published four times a year.

Websites

www.achuka.co.uk

This features interviews with children's writers.

You may also want to look at some publishers' websites:

www.hodderheadline.co.uk
www.puffin.co.uk
www.panmacmillan.com

Acknowledgements

The author and publisher would like to thank the following for permission to reproduce copyright material:

Extracts

P5 Viking Books for *The Bear That Nobody Wanted* by Janet and Allan Ahlberg
P12 Puffin Classics for *Charlotte's Web* by EB White
P12 Puffin Books for *The Twits* by Roald Dahl

Photographs

P4 AKG Photo
P22 BBC Photo Archives
P26 Corbis

Covers and illustrations

P6, p12 Puffin Books for the front cover of *The Twits* by Roald Dahl Text copyright © Roald Dahl Nominee Ltd 1982 Illustrations copyright © Quentin Blake 1982
P7 Puffin Books for the front cover of *The BFG* by Roald Dahl Text copyright © Roald Dahl Nominee Ltd 1984 Illustrations copyright © Quentin Blake 1984
P7 Macmillan Children's Books for the front cover of *The Machine Gunners* by Robert We
P9 Random House for the front cover of *The Frankenstein Teacher* by Tony Bradman
P16 Random House for an illustration from *The Frankenstein Teacher* by Tony Bradman
P12 Puffin Books for the front cover of *The Secret Garden* by Frances Hodgson Burnett 1994 Illustrations copyright © Robin Lawrie 1994
P13 Hamish Hamilton for the front cover of and an illustration from *Charlotte's Web* by EB White 1952 Copyright © 1952 J White
P14 Egmont Books Ltd, London for the illustration from the front cover of *Dilly to the Rescue* Cover illustration © Susan Hellard 1999
P15 Egmont Books Ltd, London for illustrations from *Dilly to the Rescue* Inside illustrations © Susan Hellard 1991
P17 Bloomsbury Publishing plc for the front cover of *Harry Potter and the Philosopher's Stone* by JK Rowling 1997 Cover illustration copyright © Thomas Taylor 1997
P17 Puffin Books for an illustration from *The Sheep-Pig* by Dick King-Smith 1985 Illustrations copyright © Mike Terry 1999
P21 Ronald Grant Archive
P23 Egmont Books Ltd, London for the illustration from the front cover of *Dilly at the Funfair* Cover illustration © Susan Hellard 1999
P23 Egmont Books Ltd, London for an illustration from *Dilly to the Rescue* Inside illustrations © Susan Hellard
P28 Egmont Books Ltd, London for an illustration from *The Thing That Came From Jason's Nose* Illustrations © Martin Chatterton 1999

While every effort has been made to obtain permission, there may still be cases in w we have failed to trace a copyright holder. The publisher will be happy to correct an omission in future reprintings.